DATE			

Loving

the being together books

PUBERTY AND ADOLESCENCE

CONCEPTION AND CONTRACEPTION

PREGNANCY

BIRTH

HEREDITY

DATING ☐

LOVING ☐

SEX OUTSIDE OF MARRIAGE ☐

MARRIAGE ☐

☐ recommended for junior and senior high only

We specialize in producing quality books for young people. For a complete list please write

LERNER PUBLICATIONS COMPANY
241 First Avenue North, Minneapolis, Minnesota 55401

a being together book

Loving

Jean Coryllel Lipke

Illustrated by Patricia Bateman

Published by
Lerner Publications Company
Minneapolis, Minnesota

ACKNOWLEDGMENTS

If the Being Together books give young people the answers they need to lead richer and more meaningful lives, much credit goes to those individuals who helped the author in every stage of preparing these books. Many gave freely of their time, knowledge, and experience, but my special thanks go to Robert W. Soll, M.D., Ph.D., *University of Minnesota Medical School;* Reverend Paul M. Youngdahl, *Associate Pastor, Mount Olivet Lutheran Church;* Reverend Thomas P. Hunstiger, *Pastor, St. Stephen's Catholic Church;* Adora Miller, R.N., *In-service Instructor, Fairview Hospital, Minneapolis, Minnesota;* Catherine Myers, R.N., *Head Nurse of Obstetrics, Gynecology and Family Planning, Outpatient Department, St. Paul-Ramsey Hospital and Medical Center, St. Paul, Minnesota;* James R. Bergquist, M.D., *Clinical Assistant Professor, Obstetrics and Gynecology, University of Minnesota Medical School;* Simon Davidson, *Family Counselor, Jewish Family and Children's Service, Minneapolis, Minnesota;* James Merrill, *Director of Child Welfare Division, Lutheran Social Service, Minneapolis, Minnesota;* and Barbara S. Teeter, Ph.D., *Lake Minnetonka Mental Health Center, Wayzata, Minnesota.*

JEAN CORYLLEL LIPKE

The Library of Congress cataloged the
original printing of this title as follows:

Lipke, Jean Coryllel.
    Loving. Illustrated by Patricia Bateman. Minneapolis, Lerner Publications Co. [1971]

    56 p. col. illus. 23 cm. (A Being Together Book)

    SUMMARY: Discusses the various kinds of love and their influence on an individual's growth, maturity, and choice of a mate.

    1. Love—Juvenile literature. [1. Love] I. Bateman, Patricia, illus. II. Title.

HQ10.L52   152.4   72-104894
ISBN 0-8225-0593-2   MARC
                                                     AC

51486

£1- 13733

Love and affection are as necessary for human growth and development as food and rest. Human beings need to love and be loved. Without love the human personality would be sick, just as the body becomes sick without nourishment and care. Loving is not automatic, however; it is learned. Consciously or unconsciously, a child learns to love as he grows up. There are many kinds of love and many stages in the development of love. And learning to love never stops. This book discusses the various kinds of love and how they develop. It also gives some considerations for choosing a marriage partner.

EARLY LOVE DEVELOPMENT

Loving begins at birth, but a baby first feels love only for himself. He is completely absorbed in his own feelings and desires. Of course the whole process of being born is quite a shock to him. Life in this world is very uncomfortable compared to what he has been used to. He may feel hungry, cold, wet, or insecure. So he cries until these complaints are taken care of. All that matters to him is what *he* wants. If he gets it, he is happy. If he does not, he becomes unhappy or angry. But that is all a newborn baby is aware of, just himself. He is not yet interested in other people and things.

One of the first persons to penetrate a baby's self-centeredness is his mother, or whoever answers his cries. If his mother feeds him, dries him, cuddles him, and makes him feel warm and secure, he loves her. He loves her, not for herself, but for what she does for him. She makes him comfortable and happy. He learns to trust her and feel secure with her. Real affection for her begins when the baby is around nine months of age.

7

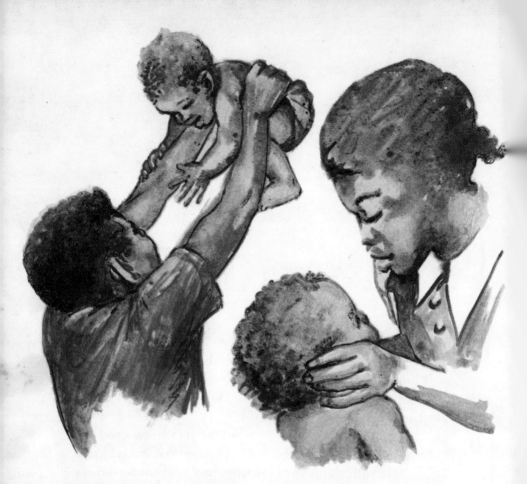

As the baby gets older he becomes aware of more people. His father takes a turn at feeding and holding and comforting. Dad represents strength and security, perhaps rough-housing and fun. Dad becomes his trusted playmate. By the time he is a year old the baby has learned to love his father.

If the baby has brothers and sisters and grandparents his circle of loved ones grows. First he feels pleasure at their attentions. They meet his demands, amuse him, and make him comfortable. He then learns to return their affection. This usually happens when the baby is a year to a year and a half old.

Children depend upon their family for affection and approval as well as physical comforts. If selfishness brings disapproval, the child learns to think of others besides himself. When a child begins to care about others and to trust them, and when he feels that they accept him, he is no longer concerned only with himself. He imitates and returns the love of others.

Unfortunately, the reverse is also true. If a child finds that he cannot trust his parents to take care of his physical and emotional needs, he does not care about his family. If he feels insecure and unloved, he does not learn how to love others. He grows up being more concerned about himself than others.

Once a child has learned to love and care about his family, he is ready to enter the next stage of love development, love for people outside the family. If a child has found affection and approval within his home, he expects to find the same from others. Neighborhood playmates enter into his circle of love and friendship. Usually one special person becomes his closest friend. This favorite pal can be of the same or opposite sex; it does not matter at this preschool age. The ways of showing affection learned in the family are used with the new friend. Hugs, kisses, and hand-holding are all part of this stage of loving. Preschool children share toys, treats, and secrets. They also play many "pretend" games.

When a child is in elementary school his best friends are usually of his own sex. Here affections are very strong, but they are no longer demonstrated by hugs and kisses. Rather, the friends are almost always together, sharing projects and activities in school and out. They are extremely loyal to one another and share all secrets, plans, and dreams. Giving and accepting this kind of love is an important step in building for future relationships with both sexes. Children need to find security and companionship outside as well as inside the family.

LOVE DEVELOPMENT
DURING ADOLESCENCE

During the early high school years a type of "hero worship" may enter into the best-friend relationship or even take the place of that best friend. Hero worship at this age usually takes the form of admiration and affection for an older person of the same sex. Some people call this kind of admiration a "crush" because these love feelings are very strong and usually one-sided. A younger child may imitate the parent of the same sex. Children often want to be just like their mother or father because they love and admire them so much. For boys and girls in junior high, love development has grown beyond the home. They find a new hero to imitate. Boys may be attracted to a doctor, minister, teacher, coach, or professional athlete. Girls look to such people as nurses, teachers, movie stars, singers, and dancers. Young teens, trying to decide on a future for themselves, often copy their hero and plan for a similar career.

14

Another form of hero worship, which usually comes later than the first, is affection for an older person of the opposite sex. Young teenagers are not quite ready for close friendships with teenagers of the opposite sex, but they are beginning to think a little romantically about the kind of man or woman they could eventually love and marry. They find the "perfect girl" or "perfect man" on the movie screen, on records, or in real life, and they spend their love energies dreaming about this special person.

16

Often, if a girl is very fond of her father, she gets a crush on a man similar to him in age, looks, or personality. If a boy is very close to his mother, he may spend his attentions on someone who reminds him of her. Or if a girl does not get along with her father, she may be attracted to a man with the opposite qualities of her dad. And a boy may become interested in a woman just because she is very different from his mother. Usually these crushes are not returned. The teenager feels love and admiration for this older person, but he really does not expect to be loved back. It is a safe arrangement that the teenager knows he can end whenever he wants to. He feels no responsibility toward his hero. The hero will not be upset or hurt if the young person turns his affections somewhere else.

DATING

In the next stage of love development, the teenager is ready to place his interest and affections on a teenager of the opposite sex. Usually this interest is first aimed at all members of that sex. The teen becomes "boy-crazy" or "girl-crazy" for a time. This is really very healthy, for it gives boys and girls a chance to look over the "field" and find out what the opposite sex is like at this age. It probably has been several years since the teenager has had any close contact with persons of the opposite sex. Brothers and sisters do not count (except that having their friends around the house may have taught the teenager a few things). Actually, since both boys and girls experience a big, new interest in the opposite sex, none of them are going to act as they used to. Everyone needs to get reacquainted. It is time for dating.

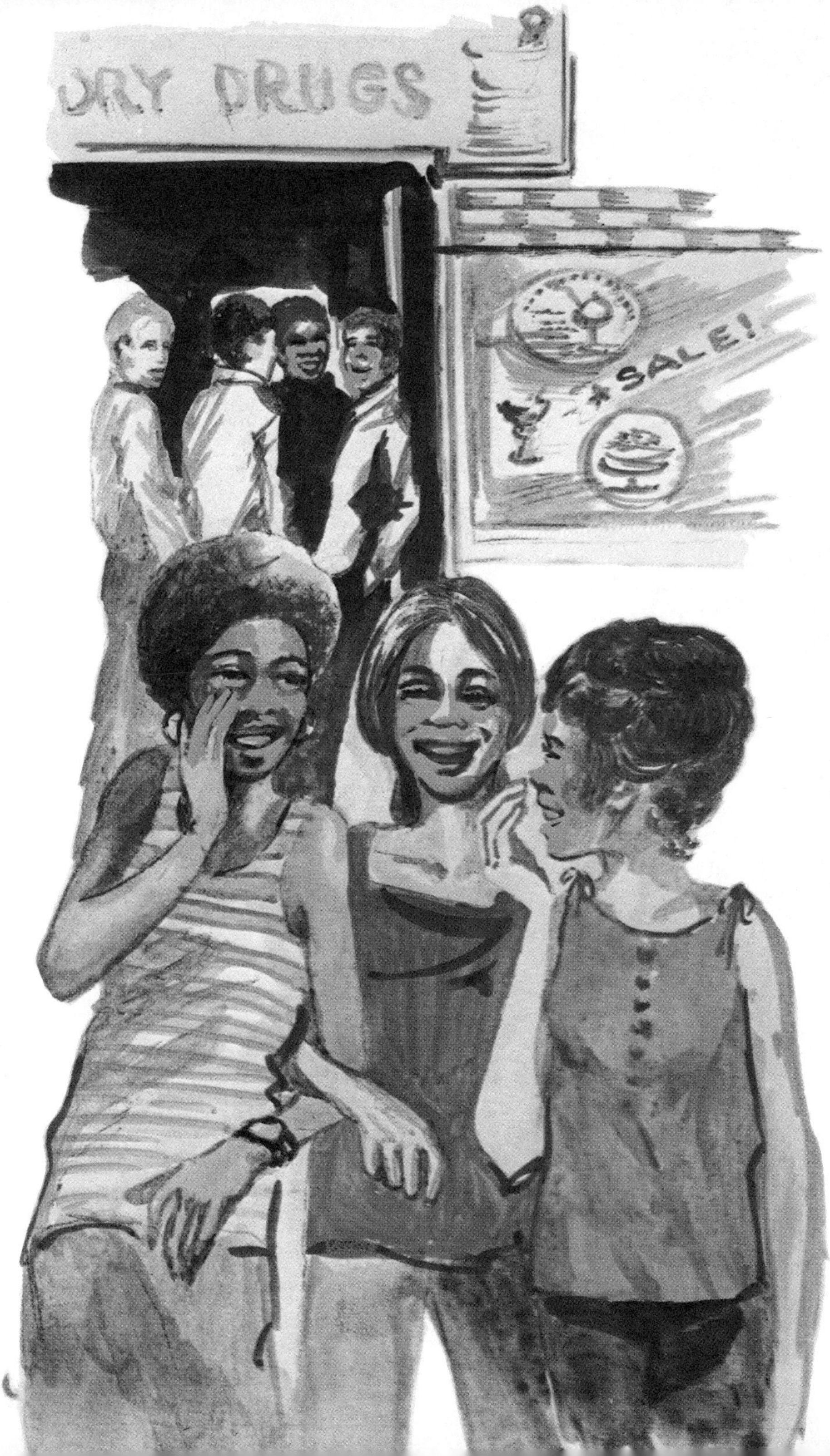
DRY DRUGS
SALE!

The most comfortable way to begin dating is to go on group dates. On a group date a number of boys and girls get together for a party or picnic, and no one is really "with" anyone else. Everyone comes "stag," or on his own. Even money-raising projects, such as carwashes, can turn into enjoyable group dates. Informal get-togethers at a favorite teenage gathering place may be another chance for group dating. Any opportunity for teens to meet and be together, either for work or for recreation, is a kind of group date. These dates help the teenager learn to relax and feel comfortable around members of the opposite sex.

The first stages of a boy-craze or a girl-craze are aimed at all members of the opposite sex, but after a while one or two individuals seem more appealing than the rest. When a fascination with the opposite sex becomes concentrated on one or two individuals, it becomes *infatuation*.

Infatuation is often called "puppy love" and made fun of, but it brings intense feelings and is very real. Infatuation is another name for the romantic "love" that popular songs, advertisements, and movies tell us about. Infatuation is something like a crush. A boy and girl fall suddenly and madly in love. They think and talk about each other constantly, call each other whenever possible, and scheme and dream about when they can be together again. Infatuation is a can't-sleep, can't-eat excitement. The beginning attraction is often physical, or as the commercials say, "because of sex appeal." The boy and girl consider each other to be the perfect date — perfect in appearance, perfect in personality — the fulfillment of romantic dreams.

Infatuation or puppy love is not the "marrying kind of love." It may develop into a permanent love in time, but it is not the real thing right away. Contrary to what magazines, songs, commercials, and movies may say, people do not *fall* in love. They *grow* in love. The marrying kind of love, like the forms of love mentioned already in this book, takes time to develop. Two people may be attracted to one another instantly, but marriage is built on more than appearances and first impressions.

Another kind of love which young people often experience is a one-sided crush on someone their own age. One teenager falls for another, but his love is not returned. Some boys and girls seem to enjoy loving someone from a distance. It is like hero worship, except that the hero is their own age and of the opposite sex. They experience all the excitement of falling in love — not eating, not sleeping, dreaming, scheming, and the breathtaking anticipation of seeing the beloved one again.

This kind of crush is a normal stage of love development, and there are many possible reasons for it. Perhaps the teenager is not ready to become involved with someone who might return his affection. Some teenagers enjoy wanting something they can't have. They find a special pleasure in frustrated love, unfulfilled dreams, and self-pity. A boy may pursue a girl and not really want to catch her. He enjoys chasing her; he is in love with the idea of love. He may choose someone else's girlfriend or wife, or the school's beauty queen. If she returned his affection, the thrill would be gone.

Girls, too, get crushes on older men or other girls' boyfriends or husbands. Part of the attraction is that such people are, so to speak, "forbidden fruit." If parents and friends would not approve of such a love affair, that may make it all the more appealing. Teenagers sometimes like to rebel, to be different. They enjoy the "sweet pain" of unreturned love.

Another form of these one-sided love affairs is less enjoyable. At the end of nearly all romances, love becomes one-sided. One partner becomes uninterested and falls out of love before the other does. This can be very difficult if the couple has been going together for a long time. The person who has been rejected suffers the heartache of love lost. He is also totally out of circulation and therefore dateless for a time. The teenager misses not only the loved one, but also all the fun and dates he or she represented. It is small comfort at the time, but nevertheless true, that their relationship probably was not the marrying kind of love anyway. Real love grows and develops. It is not something that one falls into or out of.

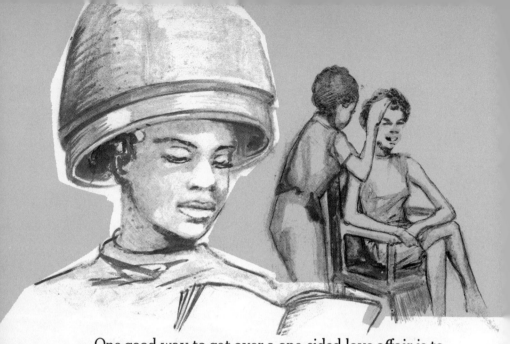

One good way to get over a one-sided love affair is to get busy and keep busy. It is wise not to allow free time for thinking, remembering, moping, and self-pity. Finding a new job, doing volunteer work, participating in school projects, improving grades, getting new clothes or a new hair style — all these will help. One should ask his friends to set up some dates for him or invite him on group dates. The best cure for forgetting an old love is finding a new one.

Usually a teenager has been in and out of love many times before he decides on the one person he wants to spend the rest of his life with. All of these relationships are important. The teenager not only learns about the opposite sex, but he also gains knowledge and understanding about himself and the way he relates to someone of the opposite sex. Until he really understands himself, he can't hope to select an appropriate partner. That is what dating is for. It is a chance to have fun, do different things, and meet new people. It gives the teenager a chance to make his own decisions and evaluations apart from his family.

One important decision a young person must make is about lovemaking. When dating becomes more serious, often lovemaking does too. Sexual love is a natural step in a person's love development, but it can cause problems for young adults. One problem is that teenagers may underestimate the power of the sex drive. Sexual desire can be an almost uncontrollable force. Boys and girls should realize that they will easily become sexually excited (*aroused*) in a romantic or private atmosphere. Teenagers who are unaware of this fact are at a disadvantage. All boys and girls have to make a decision about how far they will go in their lovemaking. Teenagers who understand the power of the sex drive can make their decision before they are in a sexually exciting situation. Teenagers who do not make a decision until after they have become aroused may make one they will later regret.

Another problem is that teenagers may mistake sexual desire for love. Sexual attraction, like infatuation, is breathtakingly exciting at first. It can be so overwhelming that it blinds a person to the rest of his date's personality. But love is more than just the body and physical stimulation: it involves the total personality. Without love, the thrill of sexual attraction is soon gone.*

*See another book in the *Being Together* series, Dating, *for more information on lovemaking and dating.*

CHOOSING A MATE

As a teenager matures, his interests change. He enjoys different types of personalities, and he goes on different kinds of dates. Once a person is out of high school, and either working or going to college, dating usually becomes more than just a pastime for fun. By this time older teenagers know what kind of individuals they enjoy being with the most, and they begin to look for a marriage partner. Many people, however, do not begin looking for a husband or wife until they are well into their 20s.

Choosing the right person for a marriage partner is probably the biggest decision a young person will ever have to make by himself. There are many people he could love and many more that he will find sexually attractive. The notion that there is only one perfect

ε/- 13733

mate for everyone is ridiculous. If it were true, what a "miracle" that so many couples found each other in this great wide world! Or, how could so many remarried widows and widowers claim happiness a second time? Human beings naturally love and need loving, and a person quite possibly could be happy with any one of several partners.

Another notion which many teenagers seem to believe is that if they do not get married *now*, they will never get married. Also false. The older a person gets, the more people he meets and the wider selection of possible mates he has to choose from. Also, as a person gets older he becomes less changeable. He is less likely to change his mind about the mate he does choose. Statistics show that marriages between adults have a better chance of survival than those between teenagers.

Some young people see marriage as the only way to gain independence from their parents. As a result, they may not choose their mates wisely. Or they may marry too soon. Ideally, young people should establish their independence before they get married. At least they should make sure that they are not marrying just to leave home.

Many teenagers ask, "How do you know when you are ready for marriage? How can you tell if you are really in love?" It is easy to be fooled. Infatuation or sexual attraction can draw two people together and send them reeling. They are almost intoxicated by the thrill of being together, just as people are in movies and magazines. Will the excitement last?

Time is the best test for love. Couples need time to really get acquainted, to share experiences, to meet one another's family and friends, to enjoy mutual interests together, to see each other in various situations, to experience unhappiness as well as joy, to share dreams, goals, and fears. If the excitement remains, the couple is probably in love.

Love is not the only standard for choosing a lifetime partner, however. There is more to marriage than romance, wedding bells, and a honeymoon. Marriage also includes seeing the same face across the breakfast table every morning, making conversation with the same person day after day for perhaps 50 years, raising children, paying bills, and growing old together. If two people have a lot in common besides their love—similar backgrounds, interests, outlooks on life—their life together will be easier.

Some teenagers look for a person who is different from their family and everyone they know. Perhaps they want to shock their family or friends by marrying someone their parents would not approve of. Almost everyone is fascinated by the unknown, the different. And most young people experience the normal teenage desire to rebel, to break away from parental ties. It has been said that opposites attract, but that is probably more true of magnets than human beings. The attraction of the opposite often fades. As the unknown becomes familiar, and as parental ties are broken, the teenager may find that he and his mate do not have enough in common to enjoy life together. Their goals might be so different that they are pulling in opposite directions. Such a marriage goes nowhere. If love is to grow and a marriage is to be successful, both partners have to help pull in the same direction.

Each partner should find the other physically attractive. She does not have to be a Miss America or he a Mr. America, but the physical appearance of each should be pleasing to the other. He should be proud to escort her anywhere, to introduce her to anyone. She should feel the same pride when he is at her side or meeting her acquaintances. They probably would not have dated or married if they had not been attracted to each other physically and sexually. This is not a superficial attraction based just on youthful good looks. It is an appeal which will last even when youth is gone.

Each should find the other mentally attractive. A happy marriage needs good communication. Engaged couples should discuss as many topics as they can think of — politics, religion, child-rearing, world events, in-laws, sports, books, art, music, philosophies of life — anything that interests one or the other. Each needs to find out what the other thinks about various topics, and how well he thinks. Not that they need to agree about everything. Disagreement can lead to healthy and stimulating conversations. But each should respect the way the other thinks. A husband will stop sharing thoughts with his wife if he thinks she is too dumb to understand. A wife will not bother to explain things to a husband she knows will not get what she means. If a couple goes stale on conversation, their marriage can be very dull. They may even have difficulty making major decisions, such as when to buy a house or how to raise children, because they cannot discuss subjects on the same level.

A difference in educational backgrounds may make mutual respect difficult. A man with an advanced degree will probably work with people having similar backgrounds. If he socializes with his fellow workers and his uneducated wife makes mistakes, he may be ashamed of her. After she makes too many mistakes, he may find it hard to love someone who embarrasses him. Education is not so important as intelligence and outlook, however. If a wife is interested in learning and stays up on current happenings, her lack of formal education does not matter.

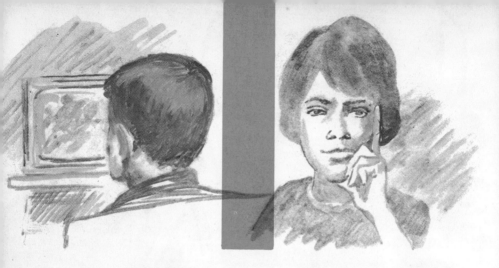

Equally unfortunate is the marriage in which the man goes stale in his job and does not expand his interests to other things. If his wife continues to grow in knowledge and appreciation of people and things, she will begin to find him dreadfully dull. If marriage partners do not find each other mentally stimulating, they may be in for some long, lonely years.

Each must also be attracted to the inner person, the "spirit" or "soul," of the other. What are his or her basic values? What does each expect to get out of life? Each should understand and appreciate the hopes, dreams, goals, and fears of the other. Their inner feelings, beliefs about spiritual matters, and concepts of right and wrong will influence their lives and the lives of their children. If they do not share spiritual beliefs, they certainly must respect each other's.

Young people sometimes make fun of married couples they see ride by in a car: "You can sure tell they are married; they sit so far apart." What they fail to realize is that a married couple has a spiritual bond which puts them closer together than any physical closeness could. This same kind of tie holds them together no matter how much distance and time separates them.

MARRIAGE

Once two people have decided that they want to
marry each other, a period of engagement gives them a
chance to make sure. Within the security of an
announced intention to marry, they can really get to
know one another. Families and friends treat them as a
couple and no longer as two individuals living separate
lives. They will spend much time together sharing plans
for their future marriage. In the closeness of an engagement, romantic love flourishes and so does sexual desire.

Married love is the next step in love development. It
is a combination of almost all the kinds of love already
mentioned in this book. Married love is part friendship,
part hero worship, part infatuation, part lovemaking.
In marriage a person loves and receives love totally —
mentally, physically, spiritually, and sexually.

In addition to all of the loving skills learned in other love relationships, married couples learn to use their bodies and specifically their sex organs to express their deep love for one another. Together they can build a closeness which no other love relationship can match. Marriage brings time and freedom to discover how best to use one's sex organs for pleasure. Each person learns what pleases his mate and what expressions of love are most enjoyable for both.

Learning to express love sexually may take time and understanding. If a person has been controlling his sexual desires for many years, he may at first have difficulty learning to relax and become responsive to his mate. Family background, religion, and education all have an effect on how one thinks about his body and about sex. There are also basic differences in desire and responses between men and women. Most marriage manuals explain techniques of loving and sexual intercourse. They are often quite technical, but most couples find them very helpful. Love and tenderness, however, are as important as technical information.

Most sources agree that there are three stages to a satisfying sexual experience. The first is called *foreplay* or "love play." The second is the actual intercourse or *coitus*, and the third is called the post-intercourse or "afterglow" period. All three stages are important to the satisfaction of both partners.

Foreplay consists of any amount and combination of kissing, caressing, exploring, words of love—any expression of love enjoyable to both. Foreplay arouses the body and prepares it for intercourse.

The second stage of sexual love is intercourse, when the penis is inserted into the vagina. After a series of rhythmic movements the couple reaches a peak of sexual excitement called climax or *orgasm*. In males orgasm is marked by the release of *semen* (sperm cells in fluid) in sudden spurts called an *ejaculation*. A woman feels orgasm as a series of muscular contractions within the vagina.

Following orgasm both husband and wife feel pleasantly exhausted. The release of sexual tension is followed by an allover relaxation. Assurances of love and affection are as important in the afterglow stage as they were in foreplay.

Like many other love relationships, sexual love improves with age. Marriage is strengthened by shared experiences, and especially by the sharing of such an intense and intimate experience as sexual intercourse. Each expression of sexual love is a total involvement and commitment of oneself to his mate. It is a selfless love which grows, rather than fades, as a couple becomes older.*

*See Marriage, *another book in this series, for more information about married life.*

OTHER KINDS OF LOVE

Marriage usually includes another type of love, called *parental love*. A person does not have to be a parent, or even to be married, to feel parental love. It is given this name, however, because it is experienced by most parents. Parental love is a protective affection, a feeling of responsibility for someone. The person wants to take care of another, to make him comfortable and happy. Some people call this "mothering" or the "mother instinct." Parents usually feel this for their children, but actually anyone can feel this way toward a loved one or a pet. It is a very natural kind of love, and it may develop at any age. Children may feel parental love for younger brothers and sisters. A childless couple may express such a love for each other or a pet. Most people experience some degree of parental love at some age whether they are ever parents or not.

Parental love grows and expands to include a wider sort of love. Many adults find that their field of love grows until it can include a great many people. Developed to its fullest, love includes an understanding and affection for all mankind. It is not a romantic kind of love, but rather a feeling of caring for one's fellow human beings. This is the opposite of the newborn baby's self-love.

Another kind of love, which does not have any special name, is the love for good friends of either sex. Even though a person has outgrown the grade-school buddy kind of friendship, he can still be friends with persons of his own sex. There are no romantic or sexual desires involved.

Such friendships are formed partly because there are many activities that men and women do not enjoy equally. Most men, for example, enjoy hunting, fishing, or golfing only with other men. Women may enjoy sewing, knitting, or shopping with other women. It is natural for people with similar interests to enjoy being together. From these associations many rich and satisfying friendships are formed. This kind of affection is as intense and genuine as any love felt for family members. Each person enjoys the company of the other; each is concerned about the health and happiness of the other.

This same kind of friendship is possible with members of the opposite sex. Just because people are married, they should not be cut off from all friendships with members of the opposite sex. Again, these are not romantic or sexual relationships. They are friendships based on appreciation and enjoyment of personality. People who work together or belong to the same interest groups or civic organizations often form a strong bond of friendship. They enjoy one another's company and are concerned for one another. It is not unusual for couples to be so fond of one another that they share dinners, go to movies or ball games, and even take trips and vacations together. Their lives and their families' lives are richer for this expanded love expressed in friendship.

A love of friends can even be stronger than family ties, especially if one lives a great distance away from his relatives. A person can choose friends to love, whereas family loves include people just because they happen to be born into or marry into the family. Single persons or persons from small families often form stronger friendships than those from large families. For them there is no automatic invitation for holidays and such. They do not have a family get-together at Grandpa's or brother Henry's, so their friends are their "family." People who have not had a brother or sister often pick someone to love like a brother or sister. Of course, people who do have brothers and sisters can also feel a sister's or brother's love for close friends. These are very genuine and rewarding love relationships.

GROWTH AND CHANGE

No two people grow up physically in the same way or at the same rate. People are also different in their love development. Not everyone goes through every stage of love at the same rate. Most people do experience each kind of love for some amount of time. An intense friendship between school-age pals of the same sex may last for several years, whereas a crush on an older person of the same or opposite sex may last only days. The time involved for each stage does not really matter. What is important is that loves and friendships grow and change. Remaining at any one stage too long could mean an unhappy adulthood.

Some people never really outgrow the first stage of love development, the love of self. This kind of person, like an infant, is concerned only with his own wants and desires. If these are not taken care of, he gets mad and pouts or throws temper tantrums, just like a baby. He always wants his own way. Some people who remain at this stage of love development are *narcissists*. They love and admire only themselves and are incapable of having meaningful relationships with others.

There are some people who never progress from the second stage, love of parents. Of course, most people do love their parents, but in stage two the love is almost entirely a dependence. The small child depends upon his parents for food, clothing, security, comfort, praise, and love. He loves them because they give him all these things and make him feel good. Perhaps neighborhood playmates and schoolmates are not so kind about making him feel good. Maybe they do not always play his games, accept his ideas, believe what he says. So he goes home to the comforting arms of his mother and father where he feels loved and secure.

If a child always prefers the company of his parents to the company of people his own age, he could have trouble ahead. If this person marries, chances are good that he will run home to Mom and Dad whenever the going gets rough. Parents are sometimes to blame for encouraging their children to remain in stage two. It makes parents feel loved and needed when their children are so dependent upon them. This is unfair to both parents and child. Neither can grow in their love development and lead a rich, full life.

To continue having friendships only with persons of the same age and sex is also considered undesirable. Normally, as a teenager matures, he begins to prefer the company of persons of the opposite sex. It may not always happen during the teen years, but usually it has happened by the early 20s. If a young adult continues to express affection only for persons of his own sex, he is called a *homosexual*. A friendship between two people of the same sex is at one age a very important part of love development and growing up. At a later age, it is considered abnormal. This is not to say that a young adult's friends should all be of the opposite sex. Definitely not. But if he places all his time, money, thoughts, and affections with a person of his own sex— just as grade-school buddies do—it is possible he is becoming a homosexual.*

*For more information on homosexuality, see Sex Outside of Marriage, another book in this series.

Some people never outgrow their crushes on older persons of the opposite sex. It is not too uncommon for young girls to marry much older men. Perhaps it is a carry-over from stage two in love development. Or because of death or divorce some girls have missed a father's love, and so in marriage they choose the strength, security, and wisdom of an older man. So, too, for the young man who marries an older woman. He may love her for the same qualities he loved in his mother. Or if he missed a loving mother in childhood, he may choose an older wife to give him the love and comfort he has so long wanted and needed. An adult marriage in which the partners are only 5 to 10 years apart in age, however, probably does not indicate any unusual love development. Everyone becomes ready for marriage at a different age.

⤲Even though a person has grown up physically and gone through the various stages of love development, he may not be forever through with them. Everyone has times in his life when he wants to return to a situation or friendship where he felt loved and secure. It is normal to slip back and forth. There are times in adulthood when a person still feels insecure and needs the comforting love and strength his parents gave him. Some days a buddy is needed to plan and dream, explore and build with, just as in school days. And marriage partners need to be lovers in the romantic sense as well as the sexual. Fortunate is the marriage in which the partners can be many things to each other.

Loving is learned. It is not an accident; it does not just "happen." It is learned from family and friends. It can't be turned on and off like a switch. Love grows. It grows out of sharing, selflessness, and a genuine interest in other people. Love given and received is one of life's deepest pleasures. Usually the more love a person sends out, the more he gets back. And there is no age limit. A person is never too young or too old for loving.

INDEX